To

From

Date

# THE FRUIT OF THE SPIRIT IS

*Joy*

HONOR BOOKS

*Tulsa, Oklahoma*

*The Fruit of the Spirit is JOY*
ISBN #1-56292-656-X
Copyright © 2000 by Honor Books
P.O. Box 55388
Tulsa, Oklahoma 74155

Compiled and edited by Paul M. Miller

When large numbers of people
share their joy in common,
the happiness of each is greater
because it adds fuel to the other's flame.

—ST. AUGUSTINE

## A BUSHEL OF *Joy*

For some of us, the major sources of joy are found under Christmas trees or wrapped in tissue that matches birthday cake icing. As a child, those were occasions when anticipation was almost as joyful as the event itself.

When childhood is left behind, dating and courtship, and finally marriage become the overwhelming source of joy, and are expressed as, "This is the happiest day of my life!" and, "I've never known real joy until now!"

But what about the joy that doesn't depend upon stuff or people—the joy that comes from God's Holy Spirit?

۶৫

According to Psalm 1, a true believer is like a fruit tree that is planted by a nourishing stream. Just as peaches are picked from such a tree, the Apostle Paul says that Christian disciples are expected to bear spiritual fruit that is nourished by God's Holy Spirit.

So now, begin nourishing yourself in the expressions of joy that you will find on these pages. Prayerfully harvest your bushel of genuine joy that is nearly indescribable and full of glory.

—PAUL M. MILLER

*In all the history of humankind no
event has ever exceeded the birth of
Christ for generating great joy.*

## HOW GREAT OUR JOY

This Gift of God we'll cherish well,

That ever joy our hearts shall fill.

How great our joy! Great our joy!

*Joy, joy, joy!*

*Joy, joy, joy!*

Praise we the Lord in heaven on high!

Praise we the Lord in heaven on high.

—TRADITIONAL GERMAN CAROL

*Some spiritual words from one of the
great English playwrights:*

## MY SOURCE OF GREATEST JOY

This is the true joy of life, the being used for a purpose recognized by yourself as a mighty one; the being thoroughly worn out before you are thrown on the scrap heap; the being a force of nature instead of a selfish little clod of ailments and grievances complaining that the world will not devote itself to making you happy.

—GEORGE BERNARD SHAW

## THE JOYFUL CHRIST

On a wall in the kitchen of the Franciscan Renewal Center in Scottsdale, Arizona, hangs a drawing of Jesus titled, "The Laughing Christ." One rather grim-faced woman saw it and asked, "Where in the Bible does it say that Jesus ever laughed?"

"Jesus was once a baby," the priest replied, "and presumably he wet his pants. Where in the Bible does it say he ever wet his pants?" The grim woman stood and left.

—CARL SAMARA

## HOW WOULD YOU HAVE LIKED TO HAVE HEARD THESE JOYFUL SOUNDS?

While the morning stars sang together . . . all the angels shouted for joy.

—JOB 38:7

## TWO DEFINITIONS

*Joy* "The emotion evoked by well-being, success, or good fortune or by the prospects of possessing what one desires."

—MERRIAM-WEBSTER

*Joy* "Remain in my love. I have told you this so that my joy may be in you and that your joy may be complete."

—JESUS CHRIST

## JOY IS NOT GUSH

Joy is not gush. Joy is not mere jolly-ness.

Joy is perfect acquiescence—

acceptance, rest—in God's will,

whatever comes. And that is so,

only for the soul who delights in God.

—AMY CARMICHAEL

## FAITH AND JOY

Even though you do not see him now,
you believe in him
and are filled with an inexpressible
and glorious joy.

—1 PETER 1:8

## THE TOUCH OF JOY

When His joy invades our lives, it spills over into
everything we do and onto everyone we touch.

—CHARLES R. SWINDOLL

## MY SOURCE

To Him I owe my life and breath,

And all the joys I have;

He makes me triumph over death,

And saves me from the grave.

—SAMUEL STENNETT

A joyful heart makes a cheerful face, but when the heart is sad, the spirit is broken. . . . All the days of the afflicted are bad, but a cheerful heart has a continual feast. . . . A joyful heart is good medicine, but a broken spirit dries up the bones.

—PROVERBS 15:13, 15; 17:22 NASB

I've made an odd discovery. Every time I talk to a genius I feel quite sure that joy and happiness is no longer a possibility. Yet, when I talk with my gardener, I'm convinced of the opposite; joy and happiness is just around the corner.

—BERTRAND RUSSELL

The most evident token and apparent sign of true
wisdom is a constant and unrestrained rejoicing.

—MONTAIGNE

There is no cosmetic for beauty like a joyful spirit.

—MARGUERITE, COUNTESS OF
BLESSINGTON

## HOW TO FIND THE JOYOUS
## WAY AS I HAVE

Ask God to forgive you.

Ask God to love you.

Ask God to take away your fear.

These are the three steps and every one is sheer

joy, because each step brings you closer to Him.

—GERT BEHANNA

## DO IT!

In Syracuse, New York, Joan E. White has organized a club called "Joygerms," whose motto is "No dues, just do." What Joygerms do is spread epidemics of joy.

## HOLY LAUGHTER

Holy laughter is a great gift of grace. It is the
human spirit's last defense against banality and
despair. Sometimes I think, that along with
martyred missionaries, comedians—those of the
gentle type—can be God's emissaries in a mean-
spirited time like ours; so for God's sake,
cultivate a sense of humor.

—HARVEY COX

## THE SECRET OF JOY

Evangelist Billy Graham tells of an old sheepherder who kept himself company playing the violin. As time went by, the old man detected his instrument was slipping out of tune. Finally it was unplayable. His solution? He contacted a local radio station and asked if they would broadcast an "A" note. The radio station staff agreed and on the requested day the old fellow tuned in and tuned up; all through the night his little cabin was filled with joyful music.

Mr. Graham then adds, "We have to be tuned to God. We will never be free from discouragement and despondency until we know and walk with the very Fountainhead of Joy."

## THE HOUSE BEAUTIFUL

The Crown of the house is godliness.

The Beauty of the house is order.

The Glory of the house is hospitality.

The Blessing of the house is contentment.

The Spirit of the house is joy.

—OLD INSCRIPTION

## THE HAPPY MAN

If you observe a really happy man, you will probably find him building a boat or something, writing a symphony, educating his son, growing tea roses in his garden, or looking for dinosaur eggs in the Gobi desert.

He will not be searching for happiness as if it were a collar button that has rolled under the radiator. He will not be striving for joy among some nebulous wastes like metaphysics. To find happiness we must seek for it outside ourselves.

—W. BERAN WOLFE,
*from A 19th-century scrapbook*

Happiness depends, as nature shows, less on
exterior things than most suppose.

—WILLIAM COWPER

## JOYFUL, JOYFUL, WE ADORE THEE

*(Sung to Beethoven's "Ode to Joy")*

Joyful, joyful, we adore Thee,
God of glory, Lord of love;

Hearts unfold like flow'rs before Thee,
Opening to the sun above.

Melt the clouds of sin and sadness;
Drive the dark of doubt away.

Giver of immortal gladness,
Fill us with the light of day!

—HENRY VAN DYKE

৵৹

A merry heart doeth good like a medicine.

—PROVERBS 17:22 KJV

Life is made up, not of great sacrifices or duties, but of little things in which smiles and kindnesses and small obligations, given habitually, are what win and preserve the heart and secure joyfulness.

—HUMPHREY DAVY

## REASON FOR *Joy*

Thank God every morning when you get up that you have something to do that day which must be done, whether you like it or not. Being forced to work and forced to do your best will contribute to your self control, cheerfulness, contentment, and a hundred other virtues which the idle never know.

—CHARLES KINGLEY

## *Joy* AFFIRMATION ONE

*Through my unwavering belief in God, I am
filled with faith and joy.*

Lord, I believe!

—JOHN 9:38

*Joy* AFFIRMATION TWO

*I celebrate life in God's wonder-filled world.*

The earth is the LORD'S, and everything in it,
the world, and all who live in it.

—PSALM 24:1

## *Joy* AFFIRMATION THREE

*I find joy in living when I share the fruit
of God's Spirit who is within me.*

Give, and it will be given to you.

—LUKE 6:38

 AFFIRMATION FOUR

*I can be eternally young in my spirit.*

Praise the LORD . . . who satisfies
your desires with good things so that
your youth is renewed like the eagle's.

—PSALM 103:1,5

 AFFIRMATION FIVE

*I rejoice and celebrate my life in Christ.*

The whole crowd of disciples began
joyfully to praise God in loud voices
for all the miracles they had seen.

—LUKE 19:37

*AFFIRMATION SIX*

*I greet each day with a joyful heart.*

You have filled my heart with greater joy.

—P S A L M  4:7

## *Joy* AFFIRMATION SEVEN

*I am filled with the joy and peace of believing
in God and His Son.*

May the God of hope fill you with all
joy and peace as you trust in him.

—ROMANS 15:13

## *Joy* AFFIRMATION EIGHT

*In my quiet times alone with God, I experience
great strength and joy.*

You have made known to me the path of life;
you will fill me with joy in your presence.

—PSALM 16:11

*Joy* AFFIRMATION NINE

*I experience a sense of joy when I give thanks*
*to God, the creator and sustainer everything.*

I will praise you, O LORD, with all my
heart; I will tell of all your wonders.

—PSALM 9:1

*Joy* AFFIRMATION TEN

*Thank you, Lord, for filling my life with*
*the joy of the Spirit.*

You will look and be radiant, your
heart will throb and swell with joy.

—ISAIAH 60:5

## *Joy* AFFIRMATION ELEVEN

*I am filled with the unquenchable*
*joy of the Spirit.*

You make me glad by your deeds, O
LORD; I sing for joy at the works of
your hands.

—PSALM 92:4

*Joy* AFFIRMATION TWELVE

*My heart sings with joy!*

You will go out in joy and be led forth
in peace; the mountains and hills will
burst into song before you, and all the
trees of the field will clap their hands.

—ISAIAH 55:12

*Joy* AFFIRMATION THIRTEEN

*My joy and gladness come from God.*

My joy may be in you and . . . your joy
may be complete.

—JOHN 15:11

## *Joy* AFFIRMATION FOURTEEN

*God's joy fills me and overflows from me to others.*

Our mouths were filled with laughter,
our tongues with songs of joy.

—PSALM 126:2

# *Joy* AFFIRMATION FIFTEEN

*Sing my soul, sing a song of joy in my Lord.*

O God, you are my God . . . I sing in the
shadow of your wings.

—PSALM 63:1,7

WHAT IS JOY?

It's basking in the Father's delight.

It's a prodigal son coming home to a father's embrace.

It's living with the pleasure of the Father's delight.

It's knowing that we are the apple of His eye.

It's believing that our stories have happy endings.

## HAPPINESS VS. JOY

Joy transcends circumstances.

*Happiness has to do with "everything going my way."*

Joy can coexist with suffering and grief.

*Happiness depends upon positive "vibes."*

Joy is rooted in hope.

*Happiness in rooted in self.*

❧

Only one thing is necessary to possess joy:
to possess God.

—HENRI FREDERIC AMIEL

## COME, WE THAT LOVE
## THE LORD

Come, we that love the Lord,
And let our joys be known;
Join in a song with sweet accord,
And thus surround the throne.

Let those refuse to sing
Who never knew our God;
But children of the heavenly King
May speak their joys abroad.

Then let our songs abound,
And every tear be dry;
We're marching through Immanuel's ground
To fairer worlds on high.

—ISAAC WATTS

## BETTER TO GIVE

God gives us joy that we may give;
He gives us joy that we may share;
Sometimes He gives us loads to lift
That we may learn to bear.
For life is gladder when we give,
And love is sweeter when we share,
And heavy loads rest lightly too,
When we have learned to bear.

—ANONYMOUS

## JOY IN THE MORNING

Sing to the LORD you saints of his;
>    praise his holy name.
For his anger lasts only a moment,
>    but his favor lasts a lifetime;
weeping may remain for a night,
>    but rejoicing comes in the morning.

—PSALM 30:4-5

## SHARE YOUR JOY

Grief can take care of itself, but to get the full value
of joy you must have somebody to divide it with.

—MARK TWAIN

## A PRAYER FOR THE FRUIT OF JOY

Father:

As your child, I am looking for more joy and contentment in
my walk with You.

I believe the Holy Spirit has planted the seed for joy in my
heart when I surrendered my life to You.

But, the seed has been slow to sprout.

Sometimes I think it got washed away in the floods of my
life. Other times, it seems like it kind of died on the vine.

Please help me produce the fruit of joy and contentment, and
may those I love see them in my life.

Amen.

*The namesake of Hasidic Jews*
*had much to say about the life*
*of joy. The following is perhaps*
*the choicest.*

## A LAUGHING FACE

There are men who suffer terrible distress
and are unable to tell what they feel in their
hearts, and they go their way and suffer and
suffer. But if they meet one with a laughing
face, he can revive them with his joy. And to
revive a man is no slight thing.

—HASIDIC

## BLESSED QUIETNESS

Joys are flowing like a river
Since the Comforter has come
He abides with us forever—
Makes the trusting heart His home.

Blessed quietness! Holy quietness!
What assurance in my soul!
On the stormy sea Jesus speaks to me,
And the billows cease to roll.

—MAMIE PAYNE FERGUSON

## FILLED WITH JOY

When the LORD brought back the captives to Zion,
  we were like men who dreamed.
Our mouths were filled with laughter,
  our tongues with songs of joy.
Then it was said among the nations,
  "The LORD has done great things for them."
The LORD has done great things for us,
  and we are filled with joy.

—PSALM 126:1-3

*From blind hymn writer Fanny Crosby; written at age eight.*

Oh, what a happy soul am I,
although I cannot see,
I am resolved that in this world,
contented I will be.

How many blessings I enjoy,
that other people don't;
To weep and sigh because I'm blind,
I cannot and I won't.

—FANNY CROSBY

Joy is not in things; it is in us.

—RICHARD WAGNER

The kingdom of God is not eating and drinking, but
righteousness and peace, and joy in the Holy Spirit.

—ROMANS 14:17 NASB

## O HAPPY DAY

Happy Day, happy day—
When Jesus washed my sins away!
He taught me how to watch and pray,
And live rejoicing ev'ry day.
Happy Day, happy day—
When Jesus washed my sins away.

—PHILIP DODDRIDGE

Rejoice in the Lord always.

I will say it again: Rejoice!

—PHILIPPIANS 4:4

## THE JOY IN COURAGE

Let others cheer the winning man,
There's one I hold worthwhile;
'Tis he who does the best he can,
Then loses with a smile.
Beaten he is, but not to stay
Down with the rank and file;
The man will win some other day,
Who loses with a smile.

—ANONYMOUS

## WHERE?
## DOWN IN MY HEART!

My memories of childhood joy? Besides the obvious ones like birthdays and vacations, it's being part of a crowd of primary kids perched on little red chairs and singing our lungs out:

*"I have the joy, joy, joy, joy, down in my heart!"*

Then all the boys would shout, *"Where?"*

And the girls answered, *"Down in my heart!"*

Again, the boys yelled, *"Where?"*

And the girls repeated, *"Down in my heart,"*

Then we'd all sing, *"I have the joy, joy, joy, joy, Down in my heart. Down in my heart to stay!"*

What did the song mean to me? Truthfully, it was an opportunity to be rowdy and out-yell the girls.

Today the concept of abiding joy is no longer only associated with holidays or rowdiness; it's all summed up in another song: *"If you want joy, real joy, wonderful joy, let Jesus come into your heart."*

—PAUL M. MILLER

## A REASON TO REJOICE

Madam, you ask why I am willing to buy your child from certain servitude and to raise her as my daughter. Many years ago a holy man bought my freedom from certain incarceration. How can I do less for the one you love? God has blessed me. He has given me contentment and an exhilaration. I am a new man. Old things are gone, and I am filled with the joy that comes from a life lived for others. One cannot serve the Heavenly Father and not find joy in doing for others.

—PAUL M. MILLER,
*Retold from Les Misérables by
Victor Hugo*

## SONGS OF JOY

Those who sow in tears
   will reap with songs of joy.
He who goes out weeping,
   carrying seed to sow,
will return with songs of joy,
   carrying sheaves with him.

—PSALM 126:5-6

## AQUINAS ON JOY

Fullness of joy can be understood in two ways. First . . . the joy of any creature must be finite. Secondly, joy is full when there remains nothing to be desired. But as long as we are in this world, the movement of desire does not cease in us, because it still remains possible for us to approach nearer to God by grace.

—THOMAS AQUINAS

## A BLESSING OF JOY

O God, in mercy bless us; let your face beam with joy as you look down at us. Send us around the world with the news of your saving power and your eternal plan for all mankind. . . . How glad the nations will be, singing for joy because you are their King and will give true justice to their people!

—PSALM 67:1-2,4 TLB

## JOY AND GOD'S WILL

Men are made for happiness, and anyone who is filled with joy has the right to say to himself: "I'm doing God's will on earth."

—ANTON CHEKHOV

## IF ALL THE GRIEFS

If all the griefs I am to have

Would only come today,

I am so happy I believe

They'd laugh and run away.

—EMILY DICKINSON

## HOW TO FIND JOY

❧

Order your soul;

reduce your wants;

live in charity;

associate in Christian community;

obey the laws;

trust in Providence.

—ST. AUGUSTINE

## AN ETERNAL SOURCE OF JOY

I have no greater joy than to hear that my
children are walking in the truth.

—3 JOHN 4

Let us fix our eyes on Jesus, the author and perfecter of our faith, who for the joy set before him endured the cross, scorning its shame, and sat down at the right hand of the throne of God.

—HEBREWS 12:2

Joy is a rare plant; it needs much rain for its growth and blossoming.

—MRS. CHARLES E. COWMAN

## NINE REQUISITES FOR
## JOYFUL LIVING

Health enough to make work a pleasure. Wealth
enough to support your needs. Strength to battle with
difficulties and overcome them. Grace enough to
confess your sins and forsake them. Patience enough to
toil until some good is accomplished. Charity enough
to see some in your neighbor. Love enough to move you
to be useful and helpful to others. Faith enough to make
real the things of God. Hope enough to remove all
anxious fears concerning the future.

—JOHANN VON GOETHE

## THE HUMAN ESSENTIALS

&c

The human essentials to joy in this life are something
to do, something to love, and something to hope for.

—JOSEPH ADDISON

## BECAUSE OF SOME
## GOOD ACT

Let me today do something that will take
A little sadness from the world's vast store,
And may I be so favored as to make
Of joy's too scanty sum a little more.

—ELLA WHEELER WILCOX

## THE INFECTION OF JOY

A baby smiled in its mother's face;
  The mother caught it, and gave it then
To the baby's father—serious case—
  Who carried it out to the other men;
And everyone of them went straight away
Scattering sunshine thro' the day.

—LOUIS DE LOUK

## GENEROSITY—A RESULT OF JOY

And now . . . we want you to know about the
grace that God has given the Macedonian
churches. . . . Their overflowing joy and their
extreme poverty welled up in rich generosity. . . .
They gave as much as they were able, and even
beyond their ability. See that you also excel in this
grace of giving.

—2 CORINTHIANS 8:1-3, 7

## FOR A DAY WITH JOY

A heart full of joyfulness,
A thimbleful of care;
A soul of simple hopefulness,
An early morning prayer.

—ANONYMOUS

## NOT JUST AT CHRISTMAS

Joy to the world! the Lord is come:

Let earth receive her King.

—ISAAC WATTS

To love is to take delight in the happiness of
another, or what amounts to the same, it is
to account another's happiness one's own.

—GOTTFRIED LEIBNITZ

❧

The root of joy, as of duty, is to put all one's
powers towards some great end.

—OLIVER WENDELL HOLMES JR.

*Jesus' Sermon on the Mount contains nine "blesseds" that might easily be translated "Joyous." Blessed is closer to happy, when in fact the word refers to the ultimate well-being and distinctive spiritual joy.*

## SPIRITUAL JOY

JOYOUS are the poor in spirit,
> *for theirs is the kingdom of heaven.*

JOYOUS are those who mourn,
> *for they will be comforted.*

JOYOUS are the meek,
> *for they will inherit the earth.*

JOYOUS are those who hunger and thirst
> for righteousness,
> *for they will be filled.*

JOYOUS are the merciful,
*for they will be shown mercy.*
JOYOUS are the pure in heart,
*for they will see God.*
JOYOUS are the peacemakers,
*for they will be called sons of God.*
JOYOUS are those who are persecuted
because of righteousness,
*for theirs is the kingdom of heaven.*

—MATTHEW 5:3-10

Five great enemies to a joy-filled life inhabit us:
avarice,
ambition,
envy,
anger,
and pride.

If those enemies were to be banished, we could
infallibly enjoy perpetual joy.

—RALPH WALDO EMERSON

Mirth is better than fun, and joy is better than mirth.

—WILLIAM BLAKE

Tired, yes, often body, heart and brain—
This then I read:
"There doth a rest remain unto His people"
and the fatigue grows less and joy kicks in,
making me believe that He came to give me rest
and life, abundant life.

—ANONYMOUS

TRUE *Joy*

True joy . . . is not attained through self-gratification,

but through fidelity to a worthy life.

—HELEN KELLER

## MY CUP RUNNETH OVER

Lisa was a junior in college. She was home for the weekend. We were sitting around the table at Sunday dinner in noisy conversation, when Lisa tapped her fork against the water glass and announced, "I want to say something." The table looked shocked—such formality. But we became silent. My daughter was serious. "I want you to know that I have made a deep and abiding commitment to the Lord."

Her mother and I looked at one another and tears instantly filled our eyes. So much prayer had been sent up for this our youngest. Before any of us could comment, she added, "I have such peace and joy, 'my cup runneth over.'" Then she looked at me and grinned. "Remember?" she asked.

For a moment I drew a blank, and then I remembered a tea party when she was a little girl. It was at a tea party when she was pouring "tea" and became distracted, and a gallon of lemonade overflowed my cup and flooded the table that Lisa observed, "I guess your 'cup runneth over!'"

—PAUL M. MILLER

No man can safely rejoice, unless he possesses
the testimony of a good conscience.

—THOMAS A KEMPIS

Blessed are the joymakers.

—NATHANIEL WILLIS

## JOY OF THE REDEEMED

❧

The desert and the parched land will be glad;
the wilderness will rejoice and blossom.
like the crocus, it will burst into bloom;
it will rejoice greatly and shout for joy.
Gladness and joy will overtake them,
and sorrow and sighing will flee away.

—ISAIAH 35:1-2, 10

REMEMBER

You do not have to be defeated—

You do not have to be depressed—

You only have to pluck a fruit from the

Spirit's garden;

Make it joy!

—ANONYMOUS

*Additional copies of this book*
*are available from your local bookstore.*

HONOR BOOKS
*Tulsa, Oklahoma*